Introduction

> *Scotland, where men are men and sheep are nervous*
>
> - Keith Mackie

Prior to writing this book, I spent two exhaustive weeks roaming the length and breadth of Scotland searching for the stereotypical view of our country.

From Lochgelly in the far north to Dalkeith in the deep south, I travelled day and night, seeking answers to a complex question. I asked first time visitors to Scotland of all nationalities, shapes, heights and sizes one simple loaded question.

When the proud nation of Scotland is mentioned what do you think of?

The range of responses (in no particular order) confirmed my preconceived expectations.

"Welcome to Scotland"

The top ten answers were:

1. Being Mean.
2. Scottish Ancestry.
3. Kilts and Tartan.
4. Bagpipes.
5. Language.
6. Whisky.
7. Football and Pubs.
8. Haggis.
9. Loch Ness Monster.
10. The Weather.

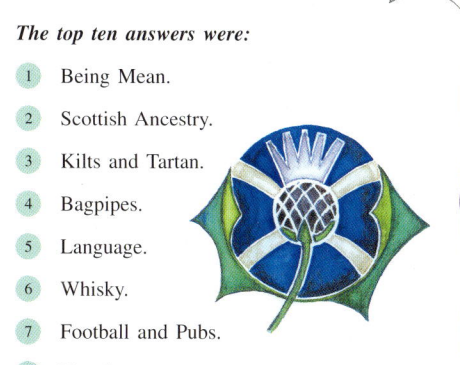

The most amusing (or disturbing) answers were: I don't speecke Engleesh; Get a life; Guinness; Lulu; Independence from Ireland; Bitten in the Trossachs by midges; The Houses of Parliament; Donald where's yer troosers; Bullocks *(I presume they were referring to Highland cattle)*; and The Bay City Rollers.

And the **TITLE?** Well, it's remarkable to think that people from the other side of the globe traverse the four corners of the earth with one vexing inquiry on their minds. It's the most frequently asked question of a kilted Scot - **What's under the kilt?**

So, this democratically compiled wee book, full of pretty colour pictures, lovely little illustrations and useless facts has been compiled to scotch a few myths, perpetuate a few more and provide the reader with an insightful and humorous look at the Scots.

Being Mean
From thrifty to frugal

> There are few more impressive sights in the world than a Scotsman on the make
>
> - J.M.Barrie

"Teabags are re-used 23 times in Scotland"

Did You Know?
In reality, the Scottish man or woman gives more to registered charities per head of population compared to any other part of the United Kingdom.

There are so many miserly jokes about the Scots - it drives us to despair. This feeling is similar to finding yourself in a round room and being told to uncover a penny in the corner. **We've heard them all before.**

This type of 'jock jibing' is what we've put up with for dozens of years. Thankfully the Scots are a well-balanced species - they have a deep-fried chip on both shoulders.

> A Scotsman went into a barber's shop and asked the cost of a haircut.
> "Six pounds," replied the hairdresser.
> "What about a shave?" asked the Scot.
> "Three pounds fifty pence," answered the hairdresser.
> The Scot retorted, "Shave my head."

The tag of being stingy was probably derived from the day to day reality of having to be careful with our food and possessions. For centuries Scotland was the poor neighbour to England *(the 'auld enemy')* and the Scots had to be canny to survive. In this day and age, Scotland has a reputation as a hospitable place full of bright cheery people. Where was this myth conjured up?

1. Copper wire was invented by two Scots fighting over a penny.
2. They heat knives in Scottish restaurants, so you don't use too much butter.
3. A Scotsman never buys an address book. He scores out the people he doesn't know in a telephone directory.
4. Scotsmen started wearing skirts because it was free for women to get into the football.
5. To avoid paying his fare, a Scot invented hiding in a train's toilet.
6. A Scot diving in a puddle to retrieve a five pence piece created Loch Lomond.
7. The most common ailment in Scottish hospitals is backache caused by locals stretching for their wallets.
8. A Scotsman goes to a wedding with elastic on his confetti.
9. If a Scotsman takes a coin out his sporran the queen blinks.
10. A Scotsman invented a cure for seasickness. He leant over the side of a boat with a ten pence in his mouth.

Did You Know?
The Bank of England and the Bank of France were founded by Scots, William Paterson and John Law respectively. Mind you, it was an Englishman (John Holland) who is credited with the formation of the Bank of Scotland.

Scotland had to ban pay-as-you-leave buses when two passengers were found dead on the top deck.

A Scottish newspaper reported:

Two taxis collided last night. Three people were seriously injured. The other twenty-two escaped with cuts and bruises.

Did You Know?

The term 'Scot free' has nothing to do with frugal Scots. The meaning has changed over the years. The word 'Scot' is an obsolete term for payment. For example, to avoid being fined in court would be getting off 'Scot free'.

In Scotland the Scottish joke is replaced by the Aberdeen joke. A favourite saying used to be, "It's so quiet, it's like Aberdeen on a flag day" - the flags relating to pins (stickers in this day and age) given out when money is dropped into a collecting tin. On the other side of the coin, the streets in Aberdeen are jam packed on 'house to house' collection days.

 A farmer and his family were trapped in their house in mid winter during the height of a severe blizzard. You could hardly see the building for snow. The Red Cross arrived by helicopter to save them, the chopper landing on the roof. One of the rescuers shouted down the chimney, "It's the Red Cross." There was a pause for a few seconds before the famous reply, "I bought one last year." Now, considering our contributions to various charities over the years, this tale pours a large cauldron of bubbling porridge on yet another Scottish myth.

What did the miserly, cheapskate, tight fisted, stingy Scots ever give us apart from trouble?

"A Scotsman finds a lost penny"

1. Telephone - *Alexander Graham Bell.*
2. Television - *John Logie Baird.*
3. Penicillin - *Sir Alexander Fleming.*
4. Chloroform - *Sir James Young Simpson.*
5. Steam Engine - *James Watt.*
6. Fax machine - *Alexander Bain.*
7. Pneumatic tyre - *John Boyd Dunlop.*
8. Logarithms - *John Napier.*
9. Tarmacadam - *John Loudon McAdam.*
10. Waterproof cloth - *Charles MacIntosh.*

My favourite Aberdeen story concerns a lady (with short arms and long pockets) who dropped a two pence piece in front of a bus. She jumped in front of the vehicle to retrieve her money and was killed outright. As she was only twenty years of age there was a post mortem examination carried out - revealing she'd died of natural causes.

 Scots and money go hand in hand. Born of a Scottish father in the British Colony of Nevis, West Indies, Alexander Hamilton (1755-1804) was the first US Secretary to the Treasury. Also of Scottish descent was James Pollock (1810-90), who is responsible for inscribing "IN GOD WE TRUST" on US coinage.

Family Trees
Looking up your ancestors

> *Every line of strength in American history is a line coloured with Scottish blood*
> - Woodrow Wilson

"Ancestral research can uncover curious relations"

Many people come to Scotland in search of their ancestors. This seems odd as most of them are probably dead. I spoke to leading Scottish gynaecologist Dr. Bryan Docherty who suggested I approach a genealogist instead. An easy mistake to make. So, I spoke to leading Scottish **genealogist** Stuart Reid who passed on to me a myriad of useless information - the type of data ideal for this sober publication. To show that my mistake was plausible, I understand that the following intriguing question was once asked, **"I'm looking for a gynaecologist to look up my ancestors"**. There's no answer to that, although a spurious operator would be tempted to take on such a challenge. Genealogy is the fastest growing hobby in the western world. This can only be good news for Stuart's company - *Scottish Roots* **www.scottish-roots.co.uk**

I asked my captive audience to name a famous Scot. The names given were an interesting mix from the past and the present.

1. Braveheart *(William Wallace)*.
2. Sir Sean Connery.
3. Bonnie Prince Charlie.
4. Mary Queen of Scots.
5. Ewan McGregor.
6. Rob Roy.
7. Billy Connelly.
8. Tam the Gun.
9. Sir Walter Scott.
10. Robert Burns. *(In Scotland he's called Rabbie, in England - Robert and in Israel - Rabbi.)*

Did You Know?

Russia was the first place in the world to commemorate Robert Burns on a postage stamp. The adhesive stamp itself was invented in Dundee by James Chalmers.

Established in 1984, *Scottish Roots* have researched over ten thousand 'family trees'. In that time, they've uncovered numerous illegitimacies, incestuous marriages, two bigamists, one poisoner and a few suicides. They've been asked to research "family trunks". In 1827 a certain Andrew Wood married a certain Agnes Twig, putting a new perspective on tracing your family tree and the subsequent branches.

Did You Know?

The first statue of an American President erected outside the USA was unveiled in Edinburgh's Old Calton Cemetery in 1893. The statue to Abraham Lincoln was erected in memory of Scottish Americans who died during the American Civil War.

Stuart tells me that he once received a phone call from a man claiming to be dead. This man wanted Stuart to find his death certificate. When it was suggested that this may be a difficult task to undertake due to the fact he was still alive, the man became very upset, slammed down the phone, and spent the next two weeks sending ripped beer mats through the post.

Apparently everyone hopes they might be related to someone famous or infamous. In the majority of cases the search will reveal a fairly ordinary list of past family members. If you're wise with the web that's world wide, and intend to look for pre-1855 records, check out this site. **www.familysearch.org**

Meanwhile, New Register House, Edinburgh, houses all statutory (i.e. post-1855) birth, marriage and death certificates for the whole of Scotland. In other words the hatches, matches and dispatches. They also hold, amongst their other historical materials, the Old Parish Registers (earliest entry 1553) and countless census returns.

Their web site is a family tree in full bloom. **www.gro-scotland.gov.uk**

On this site they have a brief selection from the Old Parish Records called *'genealogical gems'*.

Deskford, 1740 - 'Alexander Machattie in Ardoch had a child by his first wife who was born with a wooden leg'.

Shetland 1848 - 'James Robertson died 16th June 1848 aged 63 years. His death was caused by stupidity of Laurence Tulloch in Clotharter who sold him nitre instead of Epsom salts by which he was killed in the space of three hours after a dose of it'.

"Abraham Lincoln statue, Edinburgh"

In reality you can only track your Scottish relations so far back. Stuart did however have a cheery client claiming to have successfully traced her family tree back to Adam and Eve! Why she therefore required further ancestral help is anyone's guess.

```
                    Adam & Eve
                   /          \
                Cain          Abel
               /    \        /    |    \
         McCain's          MacDonalds
         /     \         /    |    \
     Robert  William   Big   Big  Big   Big
   the Bruce Wallace   Mac   Tam  Yin   Issue
      |        |        |     |    |
   Rab C.    Oor     Sir Sean Billy Connolly
   Nesbit   Wullie   Connery
```

Kilts
The temple of tartan

> ❝ I think it is possible that all Scots are illegitimate, Scotsmen being so mean and Scots women so generous ❞
>
> - Edwin Muir

Recent historical research from the artistic licence national records may have uncovered the origins of the kilt. It's now believed Ronald Macgregor, back in 1258, won a lady's tartan skirt in a raffle.

I don't think there is any other type of clothing discussed more than the Scottish kilt. The modern Highland outfit is completely different from the ancient garb. A question I've heard many a time is, **"The kilt doesn't seem to be a practical garment to wear considering the severity of Scotland's weather?"** This assumption would apply to today's kilt (made from eight yards of cloth) but the original kilt, sometimes unravelling to thirty feet, was more than practical. You could wrap your whole body in it.

"Bonnie Prince Charlie uses his equity credentials to rally his battle weary army"

Ten uses for the BIG kilt:
1. Wigwam.
2. Kite *(the flying Scotsman)*.
3. Picnic rug.
4. Hand glider.
5. Sleeping bag.
6. Big pants in case a Sumo wrestler visits.
7. Shower curtain.
8. Fishing net.
9. Bed sheet to escape from a castle.
10. Bull fighting.

The majority of people in Scotland don't own a kilt. You'll mainly see people in Scotland donning the highland dress (often hired) at evening functions, weddings, football games, rugby matches, Hogmanay or at the birthday celebrations for our national poet Robert Burns (25th January). Gentlemen also wear kilts **'cos the birds luv it'**. This is a quaint old Scottish courting expression.

There are probably more people in the New World wearing kilts and tartan than in Scotland itself. The Immigrant Scots and their offspring in Canada and North America are proud of their Scottish heritage, commemorating their Celtic roots at any given opportunity. It must be true what they say **- you can take the Scot out of Scotland but never Scotland out of the Scot.**

The earliest example of tartan dates from the third century AD. A two coloured check, named the 'Falkirk' tartan, was found near the Roman Antonine wall. The word tartan - depending on which book you read - is derived from tiretaine (French) or tiritani (Spanish) or tarsna (Irish) or tortilla (Mexican) or tagliatelle (Italian) or a mixture of them all.

Tartan has become the main symbol of Scottish culture, an emblem of Scottish descent and a modern catwalk accessory. The first tartans were simple checks coloured by vegetable dyes found in the various districts of Scotland, the colours signifying a geographical base. The clans were recognised by regional shades caused by the diversity in weaving techniques.

After Bonnie Prince Charlie's defeat at Culloden in 1746, the wearing of the kilt was banned and the Gaelic language discouraged. Anyone caught wearing tartan or playing the bagpipes could be sent to jail for six months. (The pipers should have been jailed for life.) The ban was not lifted until 1782. There was an upsurge in the 'Highland craze' after Sir Walter Scott stage-managed the Royal visit of George IV to Scotland in 1822. The king arrived wearing a kilt. Sadly, the pink tights he wore underneath clashed with the rest of his outfit. Tartan became even more popular during the reign of Queen Victoria when commercialisation took hold and tartan mania rolled on - gathering lots of moss.

"George IV"

The origin of kneeling to gauge the correct size of a kilt dates back to the First World War (1914-1918), when regimental tailors had little time to measure the troops properly. With thousands of Scots joining the British army, fresh-faced recruits were asked to kneel down in rows, so a quick kilt measurement could be taken. Nowadays, the correct length of the kilt is just cutting the top of the knee. I'm reliably informed by the infamous Highland dress supplier, Neil Manderson (www.classickilts.com) that kneeling down makes the garment too long!

Did You Know?

During the 1950s and 1960s, Edinburgh Corporation Transport would not allow a kilt-wearing gentleman upstairs on their trams, in fear of frightening the downstairs passengers.

"The tagliatelle tartan by Hamish Di Rollo"

In November 1969, Commander Alan Bean took the Macbean tartan to the moon on Apollo 12. A portion of the material was left as a flag, while the remaining section (on its return to earth) was presented to the MacBean archives. It's the **ONLY** tartan to have gone to the moon! There is absolutely no truth in the rumour that Russian cosmonauts in the 1960s trained in Scotland in a resolute attempt to acclimatise themselves to a place with no atmosphere.

With the number of properly registered tartans now running into the thousands, many businesses who want to raise their Scottish profile are having their own tartan designed. Today, tartan and kilts are part of a multimillion pound industry.

Bagpipes
Blow them up

> A true gentleman is one who knows how to play the bagpipes but doesn't
>
> - R. Acket

Question: Why do bagpipers walk when they play?
Answer: To get away from the sound.

Modern uses for bagpipes:
1. Milking cows.
2. Hot water bottle.
3. Garden watering can.
4. Boomerang that doesn't come back.
5. Car jack.
6. Television aerial.
7. Knitting needles.
8. Space satellites.
9. Fire bellows.
10. Fish bait for octopus.

WARNING — EAR PROTECTION REQUIRED IN THIS AREA

The history of pipes is steeped in mystery and legend which roughly translated means you can make it up as you go along. Real fans should contact www.kilberry.com It's often said that bagpipes are the missing link between music and noise. You either like them or you don't, there's no in-between. I fall into the latter category. I appreciate that visitors to our fine nation are intrigued to see grown men blowing into funny shaped tartan bags. However, when you've lived with a busking piper playing the same melody (out of tune) underneath your window for the best part of three long cold summers, your musical patience is tested to the hilt. My worst nightmare is the thought of being stranded on a desert island with a tone deaf piper continuously playing *Amazing Grace*.

"Better use of bagpipes"

It was rumoured that during military campaigns, pipers were sent in front of the troops to scare the enemy witless. I believe they were sent ahead of the army because their own battalions detested the bloody racket. During the First World War, five-hundred pipers lost their lives. Curiously most of them were found with gun shot wounds in their backs.

Question: What's the difference between a bagpipe and an onion?
Answer: No one cries when you chop up a bagpipe.

The bagpipes are one of the oldest instruments in existence. The actual source of this much-loved mellow sounding utensil is not known. It probably has its origins in the Middle East, evolving in Europe alongside the fusion of early civilisations. Some people say the Irish gave bagpipes to the Scots as a joke and we've missed the gag.

Apparently the Roman Army employed a horde of pipers - Nero loved them. Then again he was notorious for his cruelty, throwing Christians into large coliseums and forcing them to listen to bagpipe music.

So, were bagpipes imported and adopted by the Scots? It's possible that similar forms of pipes were invented at the same time in different countries.

Question: What do you call ten sets of bagpipes at the bottom of the sea?

Answer: A start.

A form of pipe was certainly being played in Scotland by the 1400s. This doesn't however answer the query of adoption. My only conclusion is that because Scotland is such a chilly country, much social activity takes place indoors and the bagpipes are the perfect serene instrument for the interior of a small Scottish living room.

This may cause a few Scots to choke on their rock-hard porridge - it is believed that pipes were popular in England prior to resettling in Scotland. The Highland pipe is only one of thirty different kinds of bagpipes that have appeared around the world.

"The sound of bagpipes (burning on a stove) warms the heart"

"Typical Scottish house - exterior" and "Typical Scottish house - interior"

Question: What's the difference between a bagpipe and a trampoline?

Answer: You take your shoes off when you jump on a trampoline.

Today, Scottish pipers are found busking, welcoming guests at functions or playing in marching bands.

A piper parking his car at the foot of Glencoe forgot to lock his door. Unfortunately he left a set of brand new bagpipes in the back of his vehicle. When he returned there were two sets of pipes on the back seat.

Language

Hoots man, see you Jimmy, it's a braw bricht moonlicht nicht the nicht, och aye the noo.

" We look to Scotland for all our ideas of civilisation "

- *Voltaire*

By the eleventh century Gaelic, a tongue originating from Ireland, was becoming a dominant language in Scotland. However, by the sixteenth century it was confined to the northern and western areas. A new law was passed in 1695, encouraging the setting up of English Schools in the Highlands. This regulation was a clear attempt to dissuade people from using the language. In recent years there's been an upsurge in people learning 'the Gaelic'.

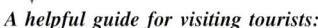

A helpful guide for visiting tourists:

1. If someone offers you a Glasgow kiss, refuse. *(It's a less than charming expression for head butting.)*
2. A free house does not mean the drinks are free. *(It's a pub not owned by a brewery.)*
3. Steamboats doesn't mean ships driven by steam. *(It's an expression of drunkenness.)*
4. A square go is not a boxed set of traffic lights. *(It's someone asking you for a fight.)*
5. A fag is not a gay person. *(It's a cigarette.)*
6. Lifted by the police doesn't mean raised in the air. *(It means arrested.)*
7. Being knocked up doesn't mean becoming pregnant. *(It's a term used to awaken someone from his or her slumber.)*
8. A Highland fling has nothing to do with extra-marital relations up north. *(It's a Scottish dance.)*
9. Being called 'hen' does not mean you look foul. *(It's a term of endearment.)*
10. A nappy is not a napkin for wiping your mouth. *(It's a diaper.)*

"A traditional Scottish evening"

Visitor: "Can you tell me where the railway station is?"

Scotsman: *(wildly gesticulating)* "Ochayenaebotherpalit'sdoontheroadandturnleftattheweehooseonthecorner."

Visitor: *(perplexed)* "Are you a tourist too?"

While quizzing visitors to Scotland, 'language' appeared in the top ten answers, not because of 'Gaelic' or 'Scots' but due to a genuine problem with understanding what locals were saying. Visitors have on occasions thought fast-spoken residents were speaking Gaelic (pronounced gallic).

"A monument dedicated to the Scottish pastime of doughnut hurling"

A useful guide to the pronunciation of Scottish place names

1. Leuchars - *Loo-cars.*
2. Edinburgh - *Edin-burr-ah.*
3. Kirkcaldy - *Kirk-cawdie.*
4. Culross - *Coo-ross.*
5. Milngavie - *Mill-guy.*
6. Dounreay - *Doom-ray-radio-active-run-fast.*
7. Kingussie - *King-ewe-sea.*
8. Gullane - *Gillin if you're posh, Gullan if you're not.*
9. Peebles - *Pea-bills.*
10. Dumfries - *Dumb-freeze.*

Ten Scottish words:

1. Cuddie - *horse.*
2. Puddock - *frog.*
3. Bubbly Jock - *turkey.*
4. Tattie Bogle - *scarecrow.*
5. Dyke - *wall.*
6. Breeks - *trousers.*
7. Minging - *rather smelly.*
8. Puggie - *gambling machine.*
9. Spirtle - *porridge stirrer.*
10. Baffies - *slippers.*

Did You Know?

The words of exclamation, surprise or disgust "Great Scot!" originated in America. The words refer to General Winfield Scott (1786 -1866) - possibly due to his notorious fussiness and pomposity as a presidential candidate.

"Going for a Single Fish"

"Tourists flock in droves to this top Scottish visitor attraction"

The lowlanders had their own language 'Scots', an offshoot from old English mixed with many European influences. The dilution of 'Scots' was hastened by the Union of the Crowns in 1603, when James VI moved his court to London and by the Union of the Parliaments in 1707, when English became the language of Government. At school, "speak properly" meant "speak English". Thankfully the culling was not fatal and large chunks of 'Scots' remain within our diction. Not only that, the lingo seems to be evolving within our own brand of English like any other living vernacular. The posh Scot thinks **'sex'** is what the potatoes are delivered in.

Whisky
The spirit of Scotland – "Slainte"

> " Whisky to a Scotsman is as innocent as milk to the rest of the human race "
>
> - Mark Twain

"The milk's for the cat"

There is always a stereotypically drunk Scot in the Hollywood movies. This isn't fair, there should be two or three. The Scots have always been seen as a hard drinking nation. Having spoken to various nationalities, I'd say several countries are in a position to claim this tottering accolade. So, who drinks the most? Scotland would probably win if we didn't export so much of our whisky.

> A Scotsman was rushed to hospital with glass and splinters stuck in his lower lip. He told the doctor he'd dropped a half bottle of whisky on the dining room floor.

It was once said that Scots would only drink Irish whiskey if they ran out of water. An old Scottish proverb states, 'Never drink whisky with water and never drink water without whisky'. In Scotland, a seven-course meal is a bottle of whisky and six cans of lager.

The history of distilling is shrouded in mystery. The process seemingly found its way from Asia to Europe via Egypt. **How's that for a vague introduction to whisky?** Looks like we set up another adoption agency to follow the successful stealing of kilts and bagpipes.

The ancient Celts produced a fiery liquid - 'uisge beatha' - the water of life. Considering the primitive equipment available at the time, the brew must have been potentially lethal - the water of putrid sheep's urine, perhaps?

Whisky can trace its distilling process back to 1494, when a certain Friar Cor took a delivery of 'eight bolls of malt... to make aquavitae'. It's hardly surprising to see a monk involved in the production of the 'demon drink'.

Whisky was at one time commended for its medicinal benefits, deemed to be good for the health. It became a huge part of Scottish social life, an ideal winter warmer and a symbol of hospitality. The Scots heat their veins from the cradle to the grave.

Did You Know?
At one time, gunpowder was used to determine the strength of whisky.

With the popularity of Scotland's spirit, the Scottish parliament stuck their big red noses in, sniffing out the potential tax revenue. Before long the greedy government were taxing not only the end product but also the initial malt. After the Union of the Parliaments in 1707, the distillers were virtually driven underground by ever increasing taxes and smuggling became a run of the mill pastime. In 1823, an Excise Act was passed making the production of whisky legally profitable.

In 1831 Aeneas Coffey developed a whisky still which enabled a continuous process of distillation to take place. This led to the production of grain whisky. The process was further enhanced in 1860 by Andrew Usher who blended malt and grain together to produce a lighter flavoured liquor. This extended the appeal of Scotch to a larger audience.

France unwittingly helped the case for Scotch. By the 1880s, the vineyards of France were ridden with disease. The French, short of wine and brandy, turned to Scotland. By the time the French industry recovered, Scotch whisky had replaced brandy as the preferred tipple.

The USA had a healthy hand in advancing the Scotch whisky industry too. At the end of prohibition, Scotland took advantage of the lack of production in the United States and exported a bountiful supply of potent liquor.

Did You Know?

The saying 'the real McCoy' relates to Captain Bill McCoy who smuggled whisky into the USA during prohibition.

"That was a strong one"

Fact or fiction?

Edward VII arrived in Scotland overnight on the Royal train. High-flying members of the railway company were to officially welcome him the next morning. It was tradition for the King to offer the reception party a dram of whisky. However among the visiting group was a strict teetotaller who was rather anxious about the impending forenoon call. Sure enough, on boarding the train the King offered all the dignitaries a dram. The teetotaller, not wishing to insult the Royal Family, quickly downed his glass of whisky with one gulp. The King looked at him admiringly and said, "What a man, have another one".

Even the American soldiers based in Britain during World War II took to the taste of Scotch, spreading the good news on their return to home soil.

Scotch Whisky is of immense importance to the economy of Scotland. The liquor is exported to more than 200 countries around the world. A true international success story.

Football & Pubs (Soccer & Bars)
Balls in the boozer

Did You Know?
The highest British attendance was in 1937 at a match between Scotland and England at Hampden Park, Glasgow. The crowd numbered 149 547.

> Our national football team don't always win, but they're often competent enough to come second

- Lorna Baxter

James II passed a law of Parliament forbidding football in 1457 as he considered the game a complete waste of time. **What did he know?**

"Scottish Cup Final 1972"

"After every Rangers and Celtic match, fans gather to exchange old footballing stories"

Scottish sport and the public house are inseparable. Although my interviewees did not specifically make this connection, the number of people referring to **"football"** was the same number who suggested **"pubs"**.

Scotland is one of the co-founders of football both north and south of the border. It was a Scot, William McGregor, who set up the English league, while Queens Park (the oldest amateur club in Scotland) pioneered the English Football Association Cup. **'Fitba'** was at the heart of many communities in the past. However in recent years dwindling attendances due to an abundance of other leisure pursuits, coupled with armchair viewing must call into question the validity of football being our national sport. It's certainly a national joke.

Only the big clubs like Glasgow Rangers, Glasgow Celtic or East Fife (Scottish cup winners in 1938) command large crowds at every fixture. Considering the amount of media attention football receives, the number of punters attending actual matches is woeful. Some of the lower division sides only attract a few hundred supporters.

Changed days since 1939 when 118 567 people watched Rangers and Celtic play at Ibrox park, Glasgow. This remains the highest attendance at a league match in Britain. Celtic were the first British club to win the European Cup and Rangers have the distinction of having the first player - Willie Woodburn - banned for life. This infamous honour was attained in 1954 when the aforementioned footballer punched Alec Paterson of Stirling Albion in the face. He didn't appeal against the Scottish Football Association's ruling, believing the ban would be lifted after a few months. Unfortunately his restriction remained in place for nearly three years, by which time Willie Woodburn was ready to hang up his boots.

Supporters are attracted to football matches by the lure of high class catering facilities available at every ground. The Saturday afternoon delicacies fulfil all of a Scotsman's dietary requirements. The nourishing menu includes mince pies (re-heated savoury mince meat encapsulated in soggy pastry), a plastic cup of Bovril (potent yeast extract mixed with boiling water) and wheel-shaped chocolate coated biscuits (filled with a gooey substance resembling marsh mallow and jam).

"Afternoon training session"

The canny Scots are good football managers. The famous Bill Shankly once said, **"Football isn't a matter of life and death. It's more important than that."**

At international level, we have the **'Tartan Army'**. This loyal band of kilted, tartan clad supporters follow Scotland around the world acting as unofficial Scottish tourism chiefs. This colourful battalion of 'football fan' foot soldiers march to far-flung lands consuming en route copious quantities of foreign beer. They have two secret weapons - humour and song. The Tartan Army's exuberant yet self-policing approach has won plaudits from footballing bodies all over the globe.

During my extensive research for this book a visitor *(clearly turning the tables on me)* asked the following question:

"If you had to create a Scottish theme bar, what would be in it?" My answer:

1. The building would be decked out with sticky linoleum floor coverings (never washed), garish tartan wallpaper and sprigs of plastic heather *(made in China)*.
2. An imitation stag's head draped in the Lion Rampant would glare down from above the bar.
3. The jukebox would play *Flower of Scotland* the twelve-inch disco mix.
4. The pub would have beer-stained unsteady tables complete with overflowing ashtrays.
5. A miserable looking kilted local would be employed to sit at the bar. His accent would be so thick, no-one would have any idea what he was saying.
6. 'Happy Hour' would be called 'Frugal Hour'. The barman wouldn't give customers change.
7. The contraception machine in the toilets would sell Irn Bru flavoured condoms *(porridge ribbed)*.
8. Locals would be obliged to provide a stunned silence when tourists walk in.
9. Staff would talk to friends while ignoring customers.
10. An empty wall would be dedicated to great Scottish sporting achievements.

Did You Know?

The world's first international football match took place in 1872. Scotland and England played out a 0-0 draw in Glasgow.

There are many exotic nationalities living in Scotland. What's remarkable is the low profile of these foreign nationals until England are playing at football. Suddenly the Scottish pubs are full of supporters, cheering on England's opponents. This is of course just light-hearted neighbourly rivalry . . . (aye right).

Haggis
An endangered species

> Upon a hill there was a coo, it must hae gone cause it's no there noo

- James XII

"Scottish cuisine"

Some people think a haggis looks like a football. They say its difficult to tell whether you should kick it or eat it. After you've eaten it, you wish you'd kicked it.

The sport of haggis baiting has become ever more popular since the 1970s leading to a genuine fear of extinction. Experts believe that if the hunting of haggis by packs of docile Skye terriers is not properly licensed, this remarkable animal could be extinct by the start of the next decade. Thankfully a group of like-minded farmers from the Haggis Organisation for Good (HOG) have implemented a newly engineered breeding schedule at an Inverness safari park. Their aim is to re-populate the Scottish countryside with this most dextrous of creatures.

Did You Know?

The sweet toothed Scot consumes a vast quantity of cakes, chocolate, sweeties and ice cream. So, to say someone has a sweet tooth is a contradiction in terms considering sweeties make your teeth fall out.

THE MYTH

A haggis is a small three-legged animal native to the Highland glens and mountains. Indigenous to Scotland the wee globular beastie is considered a delicacy amongst the upper echelons of society. Beware though, haggis is only available in season - 30th November (St. Andrews Day) to 25th January (Robert Burns birthday).

The first 'hands on' haggis birth made national headlines in March 2000, when Doctor Campbell Macdonald delivered a twelve pound eight ounce haggis in the safari park's purpose-built haggis house (known as a croft). The healthy beast, affectionately named Donald by the park's administration staff, will be a walking howling attraction in the park for many years to come. It is believed that in a loving caring environment, the Highland haggis can live for up to sixty-two years.

THE FACTS

Haggis is the following:

A savoury dish made from the internal organs of a sheep (minced) mixed with oatmeal, spices, salt, pepper and boiled in a sheep's stomach. The sheep is normally dead and the stomach removed prior to boiling. This is the ancient equivalent of a 'boil in the bag' meal. Seemingly this concoction was a popular meal in Greece before arriving on Scottish shores. Haggis is normally served with mashed neeps (turnip) and mashed tatties (potatoes). Although considered our national dish, it's not a meal you'd regularly eat. In more recent times, haggis has been found in the fish and chip shop, deep-fried in batter. It wasn't a Scotsman who invented vegetable oil but as a nation we've certainly had a go at frying every known food - including Mars bars.

The heaviest recorded haggis weighed sixteen stone four ounces, caught by an Orkney farmer in 1922.

Other Scottish grub:

1. Scotch broth - *barley and vegetable soup.*
2. Cullen Skink - *cream of smoked haddock soup.*
3. Cock-a-leekie - *leek and chicken soup served with prunes.*
4. Bannocks - *oatcakes.*
5. Scotch Eggs - *boiled eggs surrounded in sausage meat and deep fried in bread crumbs.*
6. Bridie - *minced steak and onion pie.*
7. Clootie Dumpling - *a sweet dumpling made with currants, sultanas, cinnamon, brown sugar, syrup and ginger.*
8. Cranachan - *a mixture of whipped cream and oatmeal.*
9. Arbroath Smokie - *smoked herring.*
10. Dundee Cake - *heavy dark fruit cake.*

"A family of west coast haggis (permed in captivity)"

Curiously enough, the haggis makes a sound similar to a set of bagpipes. During mating season the mountainous regions of Scotland can sound like a virtual marching band.

His knife see rustic-labour dight,
An cut you up wi' ready slight,
Trenching your gushing entrails bright
Like onie ditch;
And then, O what a glorious sight,
Warm-reekin, rich.

- Robert Burns - To a Haggis - third verse

"A healthy Scottish breakfast"

Did you hear about the Scot who walked into a bakery and asked, "Is that a macaroon in the window or a meringue?" *(or am I wrang - wrong).* The selfsame baker tried to economise by making the hole in his doughnuts bigger until he realised the bigger he made the hole the more dough he needed to surround it.

"A really sad continental breakfast"

The Loch Ness Monster
The fabled fake in the lake

> " Much may be made of a Scotsman if he's caught young "
>
> - Dr Samuel Johnson

Every year thousands of visitors arrive at Loch Ness in hope of seeing the Loch Ness Monster and perhaps catching her on film. The creature, affectionately known as 'Nessie', is a national treasure. There are still regular sightings of Scotland's beloved monster recorded by the official Loch Ness Monster web site: **www.lochness.co.uk**

Explanations are many. Perhaps she's a forgotten dinosaur? Perhaps she's an apparition? Or perhaps *she* is a he? The cold murky loch has great potential to hide a monster. If you took all the water from England's lakes, streams and reservoirs and poured it into the 24 mile, 450 feet deep (average depth) space occupied by Loch Ness, there would still be room for more.

The legendary monster is more than likely just an illusion - a classic case of Scotch mist. A whole industry has been concocted around this fabulous Jurassic beast in the form of visitor centres, boat trips, fan clubs, countless high quality souvenirs and even a Hollywood movie. Call me an old cynic if you will but I'd swear the 1930s equivalent of the shrewd business-like Scottish Tourist Board met near Loch Ness to fabricate a sightseeing delusion. A scenario so improbable, it's swallowed by millions. Our monstrous mirage plays on the side of people's minds which suggests 'there just might be something out there'.

In his biography, written around 665 (published by *Dan Press*), St Columba (521-97) was said to have triumphed over a 'water beast' in the River Ness by preventing the monster from biting a swimmer in the 6th century. Now that sounds painful. Widespread Highland belief stated that water horses or kelpies inhabited nearly every lake in Scotland. These were believed to be evil spirits that lured travellers to their death by drowning. Other Scottish lochs boast their own monsters. Next to 'Nessie' in the popularity stakes is 'Morag' of Loch Morar, followed by a batch of distant cousins in Loch Sheil, Loch Lomond, Loch Rannoch, Loch Tay and Loch Arkaig.

"The legendary Loch Ness Monster"

Did You Know?

In 1999, an Australian woman, Tammy Van Wisse, swam the 24-mile length of Loch Ness in nine hours and six minutes. She beat the previous record (held by Nessie) by twenty minutes.

Sceptics would say that sightings of 'Nessie' are caused by:

1. Wishful thinking.
2. Mirage or hallucinations.
3. Cardboard cut-outs created by local primary school children.
4. Wind and heavy rain on the water's surface.
5. Boats, submarines or cross-channel ferries.
6. Inanimate objects like tree trunks, stones, picnic hampers or old socks.
7. Creatures like otters, seals, fish, deer, birds, crocodiles or Indian elephants.
8. Whisky or Drambuie.
9. The sun peeking out from behind the clouds, casting a dark shadow on the rippling loch.
10. Real life hoaxes like Roger Plumpton from Northampton (England) who in 1978 dressed up as a green monster and swam the length of Loch Ness. Sadly his papier maché costume disintegrated in the water.

"Rare sighting of the Duddingston Loch monster"

"A recent out of focus photograph of the Loch Ness Monster"

Did You Know?

The Loch Ness Monsters is the name of a Scottish Country Dance group at the University of Dortmund (Germany).

A group of scientists in 1987, intrigued by the various reported sightings of the monster, set sail in twenty cruisers and methodically swept the loch with hi-tech sonar equipment. Plenty of fish were recorded, but there was no sign of 'Nessie'. Unsuccessful attempts to find her were also made by submarine. With each reported sighting, the mythical monster's reputation is further enhanced and despite the flimsy evidence and blurred photographs, the fascination with 'Nessie' will no doubt continue for many years to come.

The Weather
It's snow fair

> The storm burst forth with great violence, but of short duration, and spread o'er a wide district, and filled the people's hearts with consternation

- William McGonagall

We know summer has arrived in Scotland when:
1. The rain is warm.
2. People open their curtains.
3. It never gets dark - apart from night time.
4. The rain clouds are fluffier.
5. You can take off one of your three jumpers.
6. Your umbrella gets a sun tan.
7. Locals drive around in their cars with the windows open and the heaters on.
8. Craft and gift shops unexpectedly appear from nowhere.
9. Locals move down to their finger-less gloves.
10. Scaffolding appears on historic buildings.

"Scottish sun tan"

With our temperamental climate a Scot did **NOT** invent the phrase, 'saving your money for a rainy day'.

Forecasters were puzzled when the entire population of Aberdeen ran out of their houses on to the streets with a glass in their hands after an announcement that there was a nip in the air. Seemingly it was a Scot who invented the sun. He exported the idea.

The weather and its potency for discussion is something we share with our southern neighbours. It's the main topic of conversation from January to December although it's a myth to suggest that Scotland is always cold, wet and miserable.

The people might be described as that but the weather can change from time to time. Cold becomes colder, wet becomes wetter and hot remains alien.

The country wouldn't function adequately if someone somewhere at some point during the day didn't say, **"The nights are fair drawing in"** or **"the winds are getting stronger by the day"**. How much colder can it get? There's a famous saying in Scotland, **"If you can't see Ben Nevis** (Britain's highest mountain) **it's raining and if you can see Ben Nevis, it's about to rain"**. The season (amusingly named summer) normally arrives and departs at some point during the second week in July.

Did You Know?

Scotch mist is not only rain and drizzle but an expression used to point out something obvious which another person has failed to recognise.

Scotland, the nation which can experience all four seasons in one hour. We even have sub-tropical plants growing on the West Coast in the shadow of the Gulf Stream. The rain in Spain stays mainly on the plain. The rain in Scotland makes no such assumptions.